MORTAL ACTS,
MORTAL WORDS

ALSO BY GALWAY KINNELL

Poetry
What a Kingdom It Was   1960
Flower Herding on Mount Monadnock   1964
Body Rags   1968
First Poems 1946–1954   1971
The Book of Nightmares   1971
The Avenue Bearing the Initial of Christ
    into the New World: Poems 1946–64   1974

Prose
Black Light   1966
Walking Down the Stairs: Selections
    from Interviews   1978

Translations
Bitter Victory (Novel by René Hardy)   1956
On the Motion and Immobility of Douve
    (Poems by Yves Bonnefoy)   1968
Lackawanna Elegy (Poems by Yvan Goll)   1970
The Poems of François Villon   1977

MORTAL ACTS, MORTAL WORDS

GALWAY KINNELL

HOUGHTON MIFFLIN COMPANY BOSTON

For information about permission to reproduce selections
from this book, write to Permissions, Houghton Mifflin
Company, 2 Park Street, Boston, Massachusetts 02108.

Library of Congress Cataloging in Publication Data
Kinnell, Galway, date.
  Mortal acts, mortal words.
  I. Title.
PS3521.I582M6   811.54   79-27517
ISBN 0-395-29125-9
ISBN 0-395-29126-7 pbk.

Printed in the United States of America

VB 15 14 13 12 11 10 9 8

Certain poems in this book first appeared in the following
publications: *The American Poetry Review* — "Angling, a
Day," "On the Tennis Court at Night," "The Last Hiding
Places of Snow," and "The Sadness of Brothers"; *Chicago
Review* — "The Still Time"; *Choice* — "After Making Love
We Hear Footsteps"; *Country Journal* — "Kissing the Toad";
Field — "Looking at Your Face"; *Harper's* — "There Are
Things I Tell to No One"; *Harvard Magazine* — "Black-
berry Eating"; *Iowa Review* — "Fisherman"; *Kenyon Review*
— "Goodbye" and "Lava"; *Mississippi Review* — "52
Oswald Street"; *Missouri Review* — "The Apple"; *New
England Review* — "In the Bamboo Hut"; *New Letters* —
"Brother of My Heart"; *The New Republic* — "Les Inva-
lides"; *The New Yorker* — "Daybreak," "Fergus Falling,"
"The Apple Tree," "The Choir," "The Gray Heron," "Saint
Francis and the Sow," and "Wait"; *The New York Review of
Books* — "Flying Home"; *The Paris Review* — "The Milk
Bottle"; and *The Three Rivers Poetry Journal* — "Memory
of Wilmington."

. . . mortal beauty, acts, and words have put all their burden on my soul.

PETRARCH

CONTENTS

PART I

FERGUS FALLING

He climbed to the top
of one of those million white pines
set out across the emptying pastures
of the fifties — some program to enrich the rich
and rebuke the forefathers
who cleared it all once with ox and axe —
climbed to the top, probably to get out
of the shadow
not of those forefathers but of this father,
and saw for the first time,
down in its valley, Bruce Pond, giving off
its little steam in the afternoon,

pond where Clarence Akley came on Sunday mornings to cut down
the cedars around the shore, I'd sometimes hear the slow spon-
dees of his work, he's gone,
where Milton Norway came up behind me while I was fishing and
stood awhile before I knew he was there, he's the one who put
the cedar shingles on the house, some have curled or split, a few
have blown off, he's gone,
where Gus Newland logged in the cold snap of '58, the only man will-
ing to go into those woods that never got warmer than ten below,
he's gone,
pond where two wards of the state wandered on Halloween, the Na-
tional Guard searched for them in November, in vain, the next
fall a hunter found their skeletons huddled together, in vain,
they're gone,
pond where an old fisherman in a rowboat sits, drowning hooked
worms, when he goes he's replaced and is never gone,

and when Fergus
saw the pond for the first time
in the clear evening, saw its oldness down there
in its old place in the valley, he became heavier suddenly
in his bones
the way fledglings do just before they fly,
and the soft pine cracked . . .

I would not have heard his cry
if my electric saw had been working,
its carbide teeth speeding through the bland spruce of our time, or
        burning
black arcs into some scavenged hemlock plank,
like dark circles under eyes
when the brain thinks too close to the skin,
but I was sawing by hand and I heard that cry
as though he were attacked; we ran out,
when we bent over him he said, "Galway, Inés, I saw a pond!"
His face went gray, his eyes fluttered closed a frightening moment . . .

Yes — a pond
that lets off its mist
on clear afternoons of August, in that valley
to which many have come, for their reasons,
from which many have gone, a few for their reasons, most not,
where even now an old fisherman only the pinetops can see
sits in the dry gray wood of his rowboat, waiting for pickerel.

AFTER MAKING LOVE WE HEAR FOOTSTEPS

For I can snore like a bullhorn
or play loud music
or sit up talking with any reasonably sober Irishman
and Fergus will only sink deeper
into his dreamless sleep, which goes by all in one flash,
but let there be that heavy breathing
or a stifled come-cry anywhere in the house
and he will wrench himself awake
and make for it on the run — as now, we lie together,
after making love, quiet, touching along the length of our bodies,
familiar touch of the long-married,
and he appears — in his baseball pajamas, it happens,
the neck opening so small
he has to screw them on, which one day may make him wonder
about the mental capacity of baseball players —
and says, "Are you loving and snuggling? May I join?"
He flops down between us and hugs us and snuggles himself to sleep,
his face gleaming with satisfaction at being this very child.

In the half darkness we look at each other
and smile
and touch arms across his little, startlingly muscled body —
this one whom habit of memory propels to the ground of his making,
sleeper only the mortal sounds can sing awake,
this blessing love gives again into our arms.

ANGLING, A DAY

Though day is just breaking
when we fling two nightcrawlers
bunched on a hook as far out
as we can into Crystal Lake so leaden
no living thing could possibly swim through it
and let them lie on the bottom, under the water
and mist in which the doubled sun
soon shines and before long the doubled
mountains; though we drag Lake Parker
with fishing apparatus of several sorts,
catching a few yellow perch which we keep
just to have caught *something*; though
we comb with fine, and also coarse,
toothed hooks Shirley's Pond stocked
with trout famous for swallowing
any sharpened wire no matter
how expertly disguised as worm;
though we fish the fish-prowled pools
Bill Allen has divined by dip of bamboo
during all those misspent days trout-witching
Miller Run; though we cast some hours
away at the Lamoille, at the bend
behind Eastern Magnesia Talc Company's
Mill No. 4, which Hayden Carruth
says his friend John Engels says
is the best fishing around ("hernia bend,"
Engels calls it, on account of the weight
of fish you haul out of there); though we end up
fishing the Salmon Hole of the Winooski

in which twenty-inch walleyes moil —
we and a dozen others who keep faith
with earth by that little string
which ties each man to the river at twilight —
casting and, as we reel in, twitching the rod,
our bodies curvetting in that curious motion
by which men giving fish motions to lures
look themselves like fish, until Fergus' jig,
catching a rock as he reels in,
houdinies out of its knot, and the man
fishing next to us, Ralph, reeling
somewhat himself due to an afternoon
of no fish and much Molson's ale,
lends us one of his, and, shaking,
sleight-of-hands for us sobriety itself's
escape-proof shroud between line and jig,
while a fellow from downcountry
goes on about how to free a snagged line
by sliding a spark plug down it —
"Well," Ralph says a couple of times,
"I sure never heard of that one,"
though sure enough, a few minutes later,
when Ralph's own line gets snagged,
he takes the fellow up on the idea,
borrows the man's spark plug, taps
the gap closed over the line as directed,
and lets her slide, yanking and flapping
vigorously as the spark plug disappears
into the water, and instantly loses spark plug
and jig both, and says, "Nope,
I sure never heard of that one" —
though, in brief, we have crossed the entire state
up at its thick end, and fished with hope
all the above-mentioned fishing spots
from before first light to after nightfall
and now will just be able to make it
to Essex Junction in time

to wait the several hours that must pass
before the train arrives in reality,
we have caught nothing — not counting,
of course, the three yellow perch Fergus
gave away earlier to Bill and Anne
Allen's cat Monsoon, who is mostly dead
along her left side though OK on her right,
the side she was probably lying on the night
last winter when, literally, she half froze to death —
and being afraid that Fergus, who's so tired
he now gets to his feet only to cast
and at once sits down, must be thoroughly
defeated, and his noble passion for fishing
perhaps broken, I ask him how he feels:
"I'm disappointed," he says, "but not discouraged.
I'm not saying I'm a fisherman, but fishermen know
there are days when you don't catch anything."

SAINT FRANCIS AND THE SOW

The bud
stands for all things,
even for those things that don't flower,
for everything flowers, from within, of self-blessing;
though sometimes it is necessary
to reteach a thing its loveliness,
to put a hand on its brow
of the flower
and retell it in words and in touch
it is lovely
until it flowers again from within, of self-blessing;
as Saint Francis
put his hand on the creased forehead
of the sow, and told her in words and in touch
blessings of earth on the sow, and the sow
began remembering all down her thick length,
from the earthen snout all the way
through the fodder and slops to the spiritual curl of the tail,
from the hard spininess spiked out from the spine
down through the great broken heart
to the blue milken dreaminess spurting and shuddering
from the fourteen teats into the fourteen mouths sucking and blowing
    beneath them:
the long, perfect loveliness of sow.

THE CHOIR

Little beings with their hair blooming
so differently on skulls of odd sizes
and their eyes serious and their jaws
very firm from singing in Gilead, and with
their mouths gaping, saying
"Ah!" for God,
"O!" for an alphabet of O's,
they stand in rows, each suspended
from a fishing line
hooked at the breastbone, being hauled up
toward the heavenly gases.

Everyone who truly sings is beautiful.
Even sad music
requires an absolute happiness:
eyes, nostrils, mouth strain together in quintal harmony
to sing Joy and Death well.

TWO SET OUT ON THEIR JOURNEY

We sit side by side,
brother and sister, and read
the book of what will be, while the wind
blows the pages over —
desolate odd, desolate even,
and otherwise. When it falls open
to our own story, the happy beginning,
the ending happy or not we don't know,
the ten thousand acts which encumber
and engross all the days between,
we will read every page of it,
for if the ancestors have pressed
a love-flower for us, it will lie
between pages of the slow going,
where only those who adore the story
can find it. When the time comes
to close the book and set out,
whether possessing that flower
or just the dream of it, we will walk
hand in hand a little while,
taking the laughter of childhood
as far as we can into the days to come,
until we can hear, in the distance,
another laughter sounding back
from the earth where our next bodies
will have risen already
and where they will be laughing,
gently, at all that seemed deadly serious once,
offering to us new wayfarers
the light heart
we started with, but made of time and sorrow.

BROTHER OF MY HEART

for Etheridge Knight

Brother of my heart,
don't you know there's only one
walking into the light, only one,
before this light
flashes out, before this bravest knight
crashes his black bones into the earth?

You will not come back among us,
your cried-out face
laughing; because
those who die by the desire to die
maybe can love their way back,
but as moles or worms,
who grub into the first sorrow and lie there.

Therefore, as you are, this once,
sing, even if you cry; the bravery
of the crying turns it into the true song; soul brother
in heaven, on earth
broken heart brother, sing to us
here, in this place that loses its brothers,
in this emptiness only the singing sometimes almost fills.

FISHERMAN

for Allen Planz

Solitary man, standing
on the Atlantic, high up on the floodtide
under the moon, hauling at nets
which shudder sideways under the mutilated darkness:
the one you hugged and slept with so often,
who hugged you and slept with you so often,
who has gone away now
into that imaginary moonlight of the greater world,
perhaps looks back at where you stand abandoned
on the floodtide, hauling at nets
and dragging from the darkness
anything, and feels tempted to walk over
and touch you
and speak
from that life to which she acquiesced suddenly dumbfounded,
but instead she only sings
in the sea-birds and breeze you imagine you remember but which you
    truly hear
as the dawn breaks in streaks across the fish-flashed water.

I don't know how you loved
or what marriage was and wasn't between you —
not even close friends understand anything of that —
but I know ordinary life was hard
and worry joined your brains' faces in pure, baffled lines
and therefore some deepest part of you has gone
with her, imprinted into her — imprinted now
into that world which only she doesn't fear any longer,

which you too will have ceased fearing —
and waits there to recognize you into it
after you've lived, lived past the sorrow,
if that happens, after all the time in the world.

WAIT

Wait, for now.
Distrust everything if you have to.
But trust the hours. Haven't they
carried you everywhere, up to now?
Personal events will become interesting again.
Hair will become interesting.
Pain will become interesting.
Buds that open out of season will become interesting.
Second-hand gloves will become lovely again;
their memories are what give them
the need for other hands. And the desolation
of lovers is the same: that enormous emptiness
carved out of such tiny beings as we are
asks to be filled; the need
for the new love *is* faithfulness to the old.

Wait.
Don't go too early.
You're tired. But everyone's tired.
But no one is tired enough.
Only wait a little and listen:
music of hair,
music of pain,
music of looms weaving all our loves again.
Be there to hear it, it will be the only time,
most of all to hear
the flute of your whole existence,
rehearsed by the sorrows, play itself into total exhaustion.

PART II

DAYBREAK

On the tidal mud, just before sunset,
dozens of starfishes
were creeping. It was
as though the mud were a sky
and enormous, imperfect stars
moved across it as slowly
as the actual stars cross heaven.
All at once they stopped,
and as if they had simply
increased their receptivity
to gravity they sank down
into the mud; they faded down
into it and lay still; and by the time
pink of sunset broke across them
they were as invisible
as the true stars at daybreak.

THE GRAY HERON

It held its head still
while its body and green
legs wobbled in wide arcs
from side to side. When
it stalked out of sight,
I went after it, but all
I could find where I was
expecting to see the bird
was a three-foot-long lizard
in ill-fitting skin
and with linear mouth
expressive of the even temper
of the mineral kingdom.
It stopped and tilted its head,
which was much like
a fieldstone with an eye
in it, which was watching me
to see if I would go
or change into something else.

IN THE BAMBOO HUT

There would come to me the voices
of the washerwomen at the stream
where they threw dresses, shirts, pants,
into the green water, beat them,
wrung them out, arranged them empty
in our shapes on stones, murmuring,
laughing, sometimes one more forlorn
singing, a sound like that aftersinging
from those nights when we would sing and cry
for one another our last breathing,
under the sign of the salamander,
who still clings, motionless, attentive,
skeleton of desire inside the brain.

LAVA

(The Hawaiian words — *pahoehoe*, *aa*, and *heiau* — are pronounced pä·hō·ā·hō·ā; ä·ä; and hā·ē·ou.)

I want to be pahoehoe,
swirled, gracefully lined,
folded, frozen where I flowed,
a clear brazened surface
one can cross barefooted,
it's true; but even more,
I want to be, ah me! aa,
a mass of rubble still
tumbling after I've stopped,
which a person without shoes
has to do deep knee-bends across,
groaning "aaaah! aaaah!" at each step,
or be heaped into a heiau
in sea-spray on an empty coast,
knowing in all my joints
the soft, crablice-ish clasp
of aa crumbling closer to aa.

When I approach the dismal shore
all made, I know, of pahoehoe,
which is just hoi polloi of the slopes,
I don't want to call, "ahoy! ahoy!"
and sail meekly in. Unh-unh.
I want to turn and look back
at that glittering, black aa
where we loved in the bright moon,
where all our atoms broke and lived,
where even now two kneecaps gasp,

"ah! ah!" to a heiau's stone floor,
to which the stone answers,
"aaaaaah," in commiseration
with bones that find the way very long
and "aaaaaah" in envy of yet unbroken bones.

BLACKBERRY EATING

I love to go out in late September
among the fat, overripe, icy, black blackberries
to eat blackberries for breakfast,
the stalks very prickly, a penalty
they earn for knowing the black art
of blackberry-making; and as I stand among them
lifting the stalks to my mouth, the ripest berries
fall almost unbidden to my tongue,
as words sometimes do, certain peculiar words
like *strengths* or *squinched*,
many-lettered, one-syllabled lumps,
which I squeeze, squinch open, and splurge well
in the silent, startled, icy, black language
of blackberry-eating in late September.

KISSING THE TOAD

Somewhere this dusk
a girl puckers her mouth
and considers kissing
the toad a boy has plucked
from the cornfield and hands
her with both hands;
rough and lichenous
but for the immense ivory belly,
like those old entrepreneurs
sprawling on Mediterranean beaches,
with popped eyes,
it watches the girl who might kiss it,
pisses, quakes, tries
to make its smile wider:
to love on, oh yes, to love on.

CRYING

Crying only a little bit
is no use. You must cry
until your pillow is soaked!
Then you can get up and laugh.
Then you can jump in the shower
and splash-splash-splash!
Then you can throw open your window
and, "Ha ha! ha ha!"
And if people say, "Hey,
what's going on up there?"
"Ha ha!" sing back, "Happiness
was hiding in the last tear!
I wept it! Ha ha!"

LES INVALIDES

At dusk by Les Invalides
a few old men play at boules,
tossing, holding
the crouch, listening for the clack
of steel on steel, strolling over, studying the ground.

Always at boules it's the creaking grace, the slow amble, the stillness,
always it's the dusk deepening,
always it's the plane trees casting down their leaves,
always it's the past blowing its terrors behind distracted eyes.

Always
it is empty cots lined up
in the darkness of rooms, where the last true men
would listen each dusk
for the high, thin, sweet clack
sounding from the home village very far away.

ON THE TENNIS COURT AT NIGHT

We step out on the green rectangle
in moonlight; the lines glow,
which for many have been the only lines
of justice. We remember
the thousand trajectories the air has erased
of that close-contested last set —
blur of volleys, soft arcs of drop shots,
huge ingrown loops of lobs with topspin
which went running away, crosscourts recrossing
down to each sweet (and in exact proportion, bitter)
✪ in Talbert and Olds' *The Game of Doubles in Tennis.*
The breeze has carried them off but we still hear
the mutters, the doublefaulter's groans,
cries of "Deuce!" or "Love two!",
squeak of tennis shoes, grunt of overreaching,
all dozen extant tennis quips — "Just out!"
or, "About right for you?" or, "Want to change partners?"
and *baaah* of sheep translated very occasionally
into *thonk* of well-hit ball, among the pure
right angles and unhesitating lines
of this arena where every man grows old
pursuing that repertoire of perfect shots,
darkness already in his strokes,
even in death cramps waving an arm back and forth
to the disgust of the night nurse
(to whom the wife whispers, "Well,
at least I always knew where he was!");
and smiling; and a few hours later found dead —
the smile still in place but the ice bag

left on the brow now inexplicably
Scotchtaped to the right elbow — causing
all those bright trophies to slip permanently,
though not in fact much farther, out of reach,
all except the thick-bottomed young man
about to doublefault in soft metal on the windowsill:
"Runner-Up Men's Class B Consolation Doubles
St. Johnsbury Kiwanis Tennis Tournament 1969" . . .

Clouds come over the moon;
all the lines go out. November last year
in Lyndonville: it is getting dark,
snow starts falling, Zander Rubin wobble-twists
his worst serve out of the black woods behind him,
Stan Albro lobs into a gust of snow,
Don Bredes smashes at where the ball theoretically
could be coming down, the snow blows down
and swirls about our legs, darkness flows
across a disappearing patch of green-painted asphalt
in the north country, where four men,
half-volleying, poaching, missing, grunting,
begging mercy of their bones, hold their ground,
as winter comes on, all the winters to come.

PART III

THE SADNESS OF BROTHERS

1

He comes to me like a mouth
speaking from under several inches of water.
I can no longer understand what he is saying.
He has become one
who never belonged among us, someone
it is useless to think about or remember.

But this morning, I don't know why,
twenty-one years too late,
I imagine him back: his beauty
of feature wastreled down
to chin and wattles, his eyes
ratty, liver-lighted, he stands
at the door, and we face each other, each of us
suddenly knowing the lost brother.

2

I found a photograph
of a tractor ploughing a field — the ploughman
twisted in his iron seat
looking behind him at the turned-up earth — among
the photographs and drawings he hoarded up
of all the aircraft in the sky — Heinkel HE70s, Dewoitine D333
    "Antares," Loire-et-Olivier H24–2 —
and the fighting aircraft especially — Gloster Gauntlet, Fairey
    Battle I, Vickers Vildebeest Mark VII —
each shown crookedly

climbing an empty sky
the killer's blue of blue eyes
into which all his life he dreamed
he would fly; until pilot training, 1943,
when original fear
washed out
all the flyingness in him; leaving
a man who only wandered
from then on; on roads
which ended twelve years later
in Wyoming, when he raced his big car
through the desert night, under
the Dipper
or Great Windshield Wiper
which, turning, squeegee-ed existence everywhere,
even in Wyoming, of its damaged dream life;
leaving only
old goods, few possessions,
matter which ceased to matter; and among the detritus,
the photographs of airplanes; and crawling
with negative force among these,
a tractor, in its iron
seat a farmer half turned, watching without expression
as the earth flattened away
into nowhere,
into the memory of a dead man's brother.

3

In this brother
I remember back, I see the father
I had so often seen in him . . . and known
in my own bones, too: the serene-
seeming, sea-going gait
which took him down Oswald Street in dark of each morning
and up Oswald Street in dark of each night . . .
this small, well-wandered Scotsman
who appears now in memory's memory,

in light of last days, jiggling
his knees as he used to do —
get out of here, I knew
they were telling him, *get out of here, Scotty* —
control he couldn't control
thwarting his desires down
into knees which could only jiggle
the one bit of advice least useful
to this man who had dragged himself to the earth's ends
so he could end up
in the ravaged ending-earth
of Pawtucket, Rhode Island; where the Irish wife willed
the bourgeois illusion all of us dreamed
we lived, even he, who disgorged
divine capitalist law
out of his starved craw
that we might succeed though he had failed
at every enterprise but war,
and perhaps at war,
for what tales we eked from his reluctance
those Sunday mornings when six of us
hugged sideways in the double bed —
when father turned we all turned — revealed not much
of cowardice or courage: only medium mal
peered through pupils
screwed down very tiny, like a hunter's.

4

I think he's going to ask
for beer for breakfast, sooner
or later he'll start making obnoxious
remarks about race or sex
and criticize our loose ways
of raising children, while his eyes
grow more slick, his puritan heart more pure
by virtue of sins sinned
against the Irish mother, who used to sit up

crying for the lost Ireland
of no American sons,
no pimpled, surly fourteen-year-olds
who would slip out at night, blackjack
in pocket, .22 pistol in homemade armpit holster,
to make out with rich men's wives
at the Narragansett Track now vanished,
on the back stretch of which horses ran
down the runway of the even more vanished
What Cheer Airport, where a Waco biplane
flew up for a joyride in 1931
with him waving from the rear cockpit,
metamorphosed at age six;
and who would stagger home
near dawn, snarl to reproaches, silence to tears.

5

But no, that's fear's reading.
We embrace in the doorway,
in the frailty of large,
fifty-odd-year-old bodies
of brothers only one of whom has imagined
those we love, who go away,
among them this brother,
stopping suddenly
as a feeling comes over them
that just now we remember
and miss them, and then turning
as though to make their own
even more vivid memories
known across to us — if it's true,
of love, only what
the flesh can bear surrenders to time.

Past all that, we stand
in the memory that came to me this day
of a man twenty-one years strange to me,

tired, vulnerable, half the world old; and in large,
fat-gathering bodies, with sore, well or badly spent,
but spent, hearts, we hold each other, friends to reality,
knowing the ordinary sadness of brothers.

GOODBYE

1

My mother, poor woman, lies tonight
in her last bed. It's snowing, for her, in her darkness.
I swallow down the goodbyes I won't get to use,
tasteless, with wretched mouth-water;
whatever we are, she and I, we're nearly cured.

The night years ago when I walked away
from that final class of junior high school students
in Pittsburgh, the youngest of them ran
after me down the dark street. "Goodbye!" she called,
snow swirling across her face, tears falling.

2

Tears have kept on falling. History
has taught them its slanted understanding
of the human face. At each last embrace the dying give,
the snow brings down its disintegrating curtain.
The mind shreds the present, once the past is over.

In the Derry graveyard where only her longings sleep
and armfuls of flowers go out in the drizzle
the bodies not yet risen must lie nearly forever . . .
"Sprouting good Irish grass," the graveskeeper blarneys,
he can't help it, "a sprig of shamrock, if they were young."

3

In Pittsburgh tonight, those who were young
will be less young, those who were old, more old, or more likely
no more; and the street where Syllest,
fleetest of my darlings, caught up with me
and hugged me and said goodbye, will be empty. Well,

one day the streets all over the world will be empty —
already in heaven, listen, the golden cobblestones have fallen still —
everyone's arms will be empty, everyone's mouth, the Derry earth.
It is written in our hearts, the emptiness is all.
That is how we have learned, the embrace is all.

LOOKING AT YOUR FACE

Looking at your face
now you have become ready to die
is like kneeling at an old gravestone
on an afternoon with no sun, trying to read
the white chiselings of the poem
in the white stone.

THE LAST HIDING PLACES OF SNOW

1

The burnt tongue
fluttered, "I'm dying . . ."
and then, "Why did . . . ? Why . . . ?"
What earthly knowledge did she still need
just then, when
the tongue failed
or began speaking in another direction?

Only the struggle for breath
remained: groans made
of all the goodbyes ever spoken all
turned meaningless; surplus world sucked back
into a body laboring to live
all the way to death; and past death, if it must.

There is a place in the woods
where you can hear
such sounds: sighs, groans
seeming to come
from the darkness of spruce boughs,
from glimmer-at-night of the white birches,
from the last hiding places of snow,

a breeze,
that's all, driving
across certain obstructions: every stump
speaks,

the spruce needles play out of the air
the sorrows cried into it somewhere else.

Once in a while, passing the place,
I have imagined I heard
my old mother calling, thinking out loud her
mother-love toward me, over those many miles
from where her bones lie,
five years
in earth now, with my father's thirty-years' bones.

I have always felt
anointed by her love, its light
like sunlight
falling through broken panes
onto the floor
of a deserted house: we may go, it remains,
telling of goodness of being, of permanence.

So lighted I have believed
I could wander anywhere,
among any foulnesses, any contagions,
I could climb through the entire empty world
and find my way back and learn again to be happy.

But when I've stopped and listened,
all I've heard was
what may once have been speech
or groans, now
shredded to a hiss from passing
through the whole valley of spruce needles.

My mother did not want me to be born;
afterwards, all her life, she needed me to return.
When this more-than-love flowed toward me, it brought darkness;
she wanted me as burial earth wants — to heap itself gently upon
        but also to annihilate —

and I knew, whenever I felt longings to go back,
that is what wanting to die is. That is why

dread lives in me,
dread which comes when what gives life beckons toward death,
dread which throws through me
waves
of utter strangeness, which wash the entire world empty.

2

I was not at her bedside
that final day, I did not grant her ancient,
huge-knuckled hand
its last wish, I did not let it
gradually become empty of the son's hand — and so
hand her, with more steadiness, into the future.
Instead, old age took her
by force, though with the help
of her old, broken attachments
which had broken
only on this side of death
but had kept intact on the other.

I would know myself lucky if my own children
could be at my deathbed, to take
my hand in theirs and with theirs
to bless me back into the world as I leave,
with smoothness pressed into roughness,
with folding-light fresh runner hands to runner of wasted breath,
with mortal touch whose mercy two bundled-up figures greeting on a
    freezing morning, exposing the ribboned ends of right arms,
    entwining these, squeeze back and forth before walking on,
with memories these hands keep, of strolling down Bethune Street in
    spring, a little creature hanging from each arm, by a hand so
    small it can do no more than press its tiny thumb pathetically
    into the soft beneath my thumb . . .

But for my own mother I was not there . . .
and at the gates of the world, therefore, between
holy ground
and ground of almost all its holiness gone, I loiter
in stupid fantasies I can live that day again.

Why did you come so late?
Why will you go too early?

I know now there are regrets
we can never be rid of;
permanent remorse. Knowing this, I know also
I am to draw from that surplus stored up
of tenderness which was hers by right,
which no one ever gave her,
and give it away, freely.

3

A child, a little girl,

in violet hat, blue scarf, green sweater, yellow skirt, orange socks, red
    boots,
on a rope swing, swings
in sunlight
over a garden in Ireland, backfalls,
backrises,
forthsinks,
forthsoars, her charmed life holding its breath
innocent of groans, beyond any
future, far past the past: into a pure present.

Now she wears rhythmically into the air
of morning
the rainbow's curve, but upside down
so that angels may see
beloved dross promising heaven:

no matter what fire we invent to destroy us,
ours will have been the brightest world ever existing . . .
The vision breaks,
the child suddenly grows old, she dies . . .

Every so often, when I look
at the dark sky, I know she remains
among the old endless blue lightedness
of stars; or finding myself out in a field
in November, when a strange
starry perhaps first snowfall blows
down across the darkening air, lightly,
I know she is there, where snow
falls   flakes   down   fragile   softly
falling until I can't see the world
any longer, only its stilled shapes.

Even now when I wake at night
in some room far from everyone,
the darkness sometimes
lightens a little, and then,
because of nothing,
in spite of nothing,
in an imaginary daybreak, I see her,
and for that moment I am still her son
and I am in the holy land
and twice in the holy land, remembered
within her, and remembered in the memory
her old body slowly executes into the earth.

52 OSWALD STREET

for Wendy Plummer and Jill Niekamp

Then, when the full moonlight
would touch our sleeping bodies,
we liked to think it filled
us with what we imagined was
fullness — actual bright matter
drifted down from the moon's
regions, so that when we woke
we would be shining. Now,
wherever we are on earth,
in loneliness, or loneliness-
easing arms, by whatever means
stricken awake, dream, regret,
our own grunt rebounding back
from the appalled future, we three
who have survived the lives
and deaths in the old house
on Oswald Street can almost
feel that full moonlight again,
as someone might hear the slow-
given sighs of post-coitum bliss
the lover who ran off could be
breathing this minute in someone
else's arms; and we taste
the lost fullness and we know how
far our hearts have crumbled, how
our feelings too long attuned
to having couldn't bear up, that for us
three gravesides were too many
to stand at, or turn from,

that most mired of pivotings,
and our mouths fill with three
names that have lost their meanings,
theirs, and before we know it, also
ours, and we pull up more tightly
around us the blanket of full
moonlight which falls down
now from unrepeatable life
on bodies of mother and father
and three children, and a fourth,
sleeping, quite long ago.

PART IV

THE RAINBOW

The rainbow appears above us
for its minute, then vanishes, as though
we had wished it, making us
turn more carefully to what we can
touch and feel, things and creatures
we know we haven't dreamed: flutings
on a match stick, the small,
blurry warmth a match gives back
to thumb and forefinger
when we hold it into the spewing
gas, for instance, or
the pelvic bones of a woman
lying on her back, which rise
smoothed by ten thousand years
on either side of the crater
we floated in, in the first life,
that last time we knew
more of happiness than of time,
before the world-ending inkling
of what pain would be for all
of our natural going — a blow so well-struck
space simply breaks — befell us,
and we fell, scanning about,
the cleverest of us, for a lover
to cling to, and howling
howls of the damned so fierce
they put terrified grooves
permanently into the throat,
which can't relax ever again,

until the day the carcass expels
defeated desire in one final curve
of groaning breath, the misery-arc
farewelling hands have polished
before each face, a last outrush
which rises through the iridescence
of spent tears, across a momentarily
heavenly sky, then dies
toward those invisible fires,
the other, unfulfilled galaxies,
to win them over, too, into time and ruin.

THE APPLE

1

The brain
cringes around the worst
that it knows; just as the apple
must have, when those two
bit into it, poisoning themselves
into the joy
that has to watch itself go away.

No one easily
survives love; neither the love
one has, nor the love
one has not; each breaks down
in the red smoke blown up
of the day when all love will have gone on.

A little sadness,
a little more self-cruelty,
a little more uselessness. These won't last.

What will last is that
no one knows enough
to let go, everyone still needs to know
the one he or she doesn't know
all the way to the end of the world.

When lovers embrace,
sometimes their arms seem only
to be remembering the other; their heads
become heavier
with ancient understandings, that skulls shall be
moonstones
and lie broken open
under the moon, only an icy light thinking inside them.

Ahead of us
in time to come, the lost ones
already touch with even more fumbling hands,
their brains convulse
around thoughts they dread to think,
these voices of ours
lie along their arteries, lie
to the blood fleeing past, *it is sweet, take it, it leaves.*

Yes, and leaves
its leaves where they fall
with fatalistic compliance on grass
which long ago gave its stitchmarks away
to the bodies of lovers
who no longer exist, or exist
as leaves that have rotted back into the apple
still brightening its bitter knowledge above us
which only needs to be tasted without fear
to be the philosophers' stone and golden fruit of the risen world.

MEMORY OF WILMINGTON

Thirty-some years ago, hitchhiking
north on Route 1, I stopped for the night
at Wilmington, Delaware, one of those American cities
that start falling apart before they ever get finished.
I met, I remember, an ancient hobo — I almost remember
his name — at the ferry — now dead,
of course, him,
and also the ferry —
in great-brimmed hat, coat to his knees,
pants dragging the ground, semi-zootish rig
plucked off various clotheslines. I remember

he taught me how to grab a hen
so the dogs won't hear: how to come up on it
from behind, swoop down and swing it up
and whirl it, all in one motion,
breaking the neck, of course, also twisting
silent any cry
for help it might want to utter —

"give," I suppose, would be the idiom.

It doesn't matter.
It doesn't matter
that we ill-roasted our hen over brushwood
or that with the squeamishness
of the young I dismouthed the rawest of it
the fire hadn't so much as warmed and tossed it
behind me into the black waters of Delaware Bay.

After he ate, I remember, the old hobo
— *Amos!* yes, that was his name! — old Amos sang,
or rather laughed forth a song or two, his voice
creaking out slower and slower,
like the music in old music boxes, when time slows itself down
    in them.
I sat in the last light and listened, there among rocks,
tin cans, feathers, ashes, old stars. This. This.

The next morning the sun was out
when I sailed north on the ferry.
From the rotting landing Amos waved.
I was fifteen, I think. Wilmington then
was far along on its way to becoming a city
and already well advanced on its way back to dust.

THE STILL TIME

I know there is still time —
time for the hands
to open, for the bones of them
to be filled
by those failed harvests of want,
the bread imagined of the days of not having.

Now that the fear
has been rummaged down to its husk,
and the wind blowing
the flesh away translates itself
into flesh and the flesh
streams in its reveries on the wind.

I remember those summer nights
when I was young and empty,
when I lay through the darkness
wanting, wanting,
knowing
I would have nothing of anything I wanted —
that total craving
that hollows the heart out irreversibly.

So it surprises me now to hear
the steps of my life following me —
so much of it gone
it returns, everything that drove me crazy
comes back, blessing the misery
of each step it took me into the world;

as though a prayer had ended
and the changed
air between the palms goes free
to become the glitter
on common things that inexplicably shine.

And all the old voices,
which once made broken-off, choked, parrot-incoherences,
speak again,
this time on the palatum cordis, all of them
saying there is time, still time,
for those who can groan
to sing,
for those who can sing to heal themselves.

THERE ARE THINGS I TELL TO NO ONE

1

There are things I tell to no one.
Those close to me might think
I was sad, and try to comfort me, or become sad themselves.
At such times I go off alone, in silence, as if listening for God.

2

I say "God"; I believe,
rather, in a music of grace
that we hear, sometimes, playing to us
from the other side of happiness.
When we hear it, when it flows
through our bodies, it lets us live
these days lighted by their vanity
worshipping — as the other animals do,
who live and die in the spirit
of the end — that backward-spreading
brightness. And it speaks in notes struck
or caressed or blown or plucked
off our own bodies: *remember*
existence already remembers
the flush upon it you will have been,
you who have reached out ahead
and taken up some of the black dust
we become, souvenir
which glitters already in the bones of your hand.

3

Just as the supreme cry
of joy, the cry of orgasm, also has a ghastliness to it,
as though it touched forward
into the chaos where we break apart, so the death-groan
sounding into us from another direction carries us back
to our first world, so that the one
whose mouth acids up with it remembers
how oddly fearless he felt
at first imagining the dead,
at first seeing the grandmother or grandfather sitting only yesterday
on the once cluttered, now sadly tidy porch,
that little boned body drowsing almost unobserved into the
    agreement to die.

4

Brothers and sisters;
lovers and children;
great mothers and grand fathers
whose love-times have been cut
already into stone; great
grand fœtuses spelling
the past again into the flesh's waters:
can you bless — or not curse —
whatever struggles to stay alive
on this planet of struggles?
The nagleria eating the convolutions
from the black pulp of thought,
or the spirochete rotting down
the last temples of Eros, the last god?

Then the last cry in the throat
or only dreamed into it
by its threads too wasted to cry
will be but an ardent note

of gratefulness so intense
it disappears into that music
which carries our time on earth away
on the great catafalque
of spine marrowed with god's-flesh,
thighs bruised by the blue flower,
pelvis that makes angels shiver to know down here we mortals make
    love with our bones.

5

In this spirit
and from this spirit, I have learned to speak
of these things, which once I brooded on in silence,
these wishes to live
and to die
in gratefulness, if in no other virtue.

For when the music sounds,
sometimes, late at night, its faint
clear breath blowing
through the thinning walls of the darkness,
I do not feel sad, I do not miss the future or need to be comforted.

Yes, I want to live forever.
I am like everyone. But when I hear
that breath coming through the walls,
grace-notes blown
out of the wormed-out bones,
music that their memory of blood
plucks from the straitened arteries,
that the hard cock and soaked cunt
caressed from each other
in the holy days of their vanity,
that the two hearts drummed
out of their ribs together,
the hearts that know everything (and even

the little knowledge they can leave
stays, to be the light of this house),

then it is not so difficult
to go out, to turn and face
the spaces which gather into one sound, I know now, the singing
of mortal lives, waves of spent existence
which flow toward, and toward, and on which we flow
and grow drowsy and become fearless again.

PONT NEUF AT NIGHTFALL

Just now a sprinkling
of rain begins. It brings with it
an impression of more lasting existence —
brings it by removal, by the swiftness
of each drop's drying from the stone.
(Soon the stone will be completely wet.
When *our* stone became wet, that was
when desolation came into the world.)
We can't grasp our debt
to the old masters who heaped up
these stones into palaces,
arches, spires, into a grace
that is beyond us, being behind us.
But we pay them some envy, we imagine
a memory filled almost completely
with what is, without room
for longing backward; and pay them
some sadness, sadness which
comes back and tries to restore us,
being the knowledge that happiness
is not here but
that it exists, even if out of reach forever.
A girl walks by, a presence
in someone's memory, and she is
smiling, clasping flowers
and trailing their odor and the memory
of her smile into the brief past
which follows closely behind.
A light comes on very dim in a hotel

window. Possibly it is a last portion
of what was once
the light of the world. In a tiny room
overlooking a bridge and a dark river, that would be
where it could come on: a dim
past-light
hovers over a narrow bed
where a girl and a boy give themselves
into time, and memory, which affirms time,
lights their moment
all the way to the end of memory.

THE APPLE TREE

I remember this tree,
its white flowers all unfallen.
It's the fall, the unfallen apples
hold their brightness
a little longer into the blue air, hold the dream
they can be brighter.

We create without turning,
without looking back, without ever
really knowing we create.
Having tasted
the first flower of the first spring
we go on,
we don't turn again
until we touch the last flower of the last spring.

And that day, fondling
each grain one more time, like the overturned hourglass,
we die
of the return-streaming of everything we have lived.

When the fallen apple rolls
into the grass, the apple worm
stops, then goes
all the way through and looks out
at the creation unopposed, the world
made entirely of lovers.

Or else there is no such thing as memory,
or else there are only the empty branches,

only the blossoms upon them,
only the apples,
that still grow full,
that still fail into brightness,
that still invent past their own decay the dream
they can be brighter,
that still
that still

The one who holds still and looks out,
alone
of all of us, that one may die mostly of happiness.

THE MILK BOTTLE

A tiny creature moves
through the tide pool, holding up
its little fortress foretelling
our tragedies; another clamps
itself down to the stone. A sea anemone
sucks at my finger, mildly, I can just
feel it, though it may mean to kill — no,
it would probably say, to eat
and flow, for all these creatures
even half made of stone seem to thrill
to altered existences. As do we ourselves,
who advance so far, then stop, then creep
a little, stop again, suddenly gasp — breath
is the bright shell
of our life-wish encasing us — gasp
it all back in, on seeing that any time
would be OK
to go, to vanish back into all things — as when
lovers wake up at night and see
they both are crying and think, *Yes,*
but it doesn't matter, already
we will have lived forever. And yes,
if we could do that: separate out
time from happiness, remove
the molecules scattered
throughout our flesh that remember, skim them off,
throw them at non-conscious things,
who may even crave them . . . It's funny,
I imagine I can actually remember one certain

quart of milk which has just finished clinking
against three of its brethren
in the milkman's great hand and stands,
freeing itself from itself, on the rotting
doorstep in Pawtucket circa 1932,
to be picked up and taken inside
by one in whom time hasn't yet completely
woven all its tangles, and not ever set down . . .
So that here, by the tide pool,
where a sea eagle rings its glass voice
above us, I remember myself back there,
and first dreams easily untangling
themselves rise in me, flow from me in waves,
as if they felt ready now to be fulfilled
out there where there is nothing.
The old bottle will shatter no one knows when
in the decay of its music, the sea eagle
will cry itself back down into the sea
the sea's creatures transfigure over and over.
Look. Everything has changed.
Ahead of us the meantime is overflowing.
Around us its own almost-invisibility
streams and sparkles over everything.

FLYING HOME

1

It is good for strangers
of few nights to love each other
(as she and I did, eighteen years ago,
strangers of a single night)
and merge in natural rapture —
though it isn't exactly *each other*
but through each other some
force in existence they don't acknowledge
yet propitiate, no matter where,
in the least faithful of beds,
and by the quick dopplering of horns
of trucks plunging down Delancey,
and next to the iron rumblings
of outlived technology, subways up for air,
which blunder past every ten minutes
and botch the TV screen in the next apartment,
where the man in his beer
has to get up from his chair over and over
to soothe the bewildered jerking
things dance with internally,
and under the dead-light of neon,
and among the mating of cockroaches,
and *like* the mating of cockroaches
who were etched before the daybreak
of the gods with compulsions to repeat
that drive them, too, to union
by starlight, without will or choice.

It is also good — and harder —
for lovers who live many years together
to feel their way toward
the one they know completely
and don't ever quite know,
and to be with each other
and to increase what light may shine
in their ashes and let it go out
toward the other, and to need
the whole presence of the other
so badly that the two together
wrench their souls from the future
in which each mostly wanders alone
and in this familiar-strange room,
for this night which lives
amid daily life past and to come
and lights it, find they hold,
perhaps shimmering a little,
or perhaps almost spectral, only the loved
other in their arms.

2

Flying home, looking about
in this swollen airplane, every seat
of it squashed full with one of us,
it occurs to me I might be the luckiest
in this planeload of the species;

for earlier,
in the airport men's room, seeing
the middleaged men my age,
as they washed their hands after touching
their penises — when it might have been more in accord
with the lost order to wash first, then touch —
peer into the mirror
and then stand back, as if asking, who is this?

I could only think
that one looks relieved to be getting away,
that one dreads going where he goes;

while as for me, at the very same moment
I feel regret at leaving
and happiness to be flying home.

3

As this plane dragging
its track of used ozone half the world long
thrusts some four hundred of us
toward places where actual known people
live and may wait,
we diminish down into our seats,
disappeared into novels of lives clearer than ours,
and yet we do not forget for a moment
the life down there, the doorway each will soon enter:
where I will meet her again
and know her again,
dark radiance with, and then mostly without, the stars.

Very likely she has always understood
what I have slowly learned
and which only now, after being away, almost as far away
as one can get on this globe, almost
as far as thoughts can carry — yet still in her presence,
still surrounded not so much by reminders of her
as by things she had already reminded me of,
shadows of her
cast forward and waiting — can I try to express:

that love is hard,
that while many good things are easy, true love is not,
because love is first of all a power,
its own power,

which continually must make its way forward, from night
into day, from transcending union always forward into difficult day.

And as the plane descends, it comes to me,
in the space
where tears stream down across the stars,
tears fallen on the actual earth
where their shining is what we call spirit,
that once the lover
recognizes the other, knows for the first time
what is most to be valued in another,
from then on, love is very much like courage,
perhaps it *is* courage, and even
perhaps
only courage. Squashed
out of old selves, smearing the darkness
of expectation across experience, all of us little
thinkers it brings home having similar thoughts
of landing to the imponderable world,
the transcontinental airliner,
resisting its huge weight down, comes in almost lightly,
to where
with sudden, tiny, white puffs and long, black, rubberish smears
all its tires *know* the home ground.